The Compass Rose

8 Ways to Awaken your Creativity and Re-Source your Life and Practice

Practice Workbook and Journal

Elaine Patterson & Karyn Prentice

The Compass Rose

Copyright © 2024 Elaine Patterson/Karyn Prentice

All rights reserved. No part of this publication may be reproduced, distributed, or transmitted in any form or by any means, including photocopying, recording, or other electronic or mechanical methods, without the prior written permission of the publisher, except in the case of brief quotations embodied in critical reviews and certain other noncommercial uses permitted by copyright law.

ISBN: 978-1-9162-5052-9 (Paperback)

First printing edition 2024.

We dedicate this Workbook to anyone who has ever wondered how they might bring a little more creativity into their lives.

Our grateful thanks also to everyone we have met on our own creative journeys. Each of you – in your own unique way – has joyfully and lovingly inspired us. We want to thank you from the bottom of our hearts for the gifts you have given us.

Contents

Welcome! 1

How to Use this Book 3

Before you Begin 7

Visiting the Eight Cardinal Points of The Compass Rose 9

Harvesting 27

Your Onward Journey 29

References, Further Resources and Reading 30

About Elaine and Karyn 35

Your creativity is waiting for you like a dancing partner.

Barbara Shea[1]

Welcome!

Welcome to *The Compass Rose – 8 Ways to Awaken your Creativity and Re-Source your Life and your Practice*. This Workbook is a doorway to prioritising your growth. It focuses on what we call 'the work before the work'.

The Compass Rose – and its eight cardinal points – contains the key foundations for starting, growing and sustaining a vibrant creative practice. It can be applied wherever you are in your life. This Workbook draws from our own experiences of learning to joyfully and wholeheartedly befriend our own creativity as well as referring to programmes we have designed and offered to international audiences. We warmly invite you to journey with us so that you too can find the hope and joy available when you dare to unleash your creativity.

We believe that we are all innately creative but that this can get sidelined due to the many pressures that we attend to and the many demands upon our time. The sheer quantity of information and data we sift through may give us few opportunities to just 'be with' the moment. Then there are the stories that we tell ourselves – that we are 'not creative' or that 'creativity is an indulgence' and / or 'creativity is not real or serious work'. We might also think that creativity is reserved for the artists who have the luxury of a studio or turret to lock themselves away in and keep the world at bay. This is erroneous. In fact, we believe that we all have an artistry we can express in our own way. We are creating every moment of every day, whether we are thinking of what to make for dinner, choosing an alternative route to get somewhere, or preparing a good answer to a sensitive and fragile question.

The 'Compass Rose' in an invitation to stop and check in with your creativity today, at this moment and going forward. Our heart's desire is to liberate everyone's creativity.

The eight cardinal points of our process are merely invitations to explore – in different ways – how you can refresh, renew or re-ignite your means of creative expression in everyday life and work. This Workbook and Reflective Journal is an ideal place to gather your thoughts as you make your way through the invitations. We hope it will launch you into a creative space where you can find the next direction for yourself. This may be in terms of your thinking or your identification of your next project or priority. You may also wish to personalise the Compass for yourself – and your clients. Build up your store cupboard of supporting invitations and practices.

How do we more consciously create what we want or desire? We stop and see where we are first, and go from there.

We would love to hear from you about your experience using The Compass Rose. Please do get in touch.

Our warmest wishes for your journey…

Elaine Patterson and Karyn Prentice from PattersonPrenticeDesigns

How to Use this Book

*I write entirely to find out what's on my mind,
what I'm thinking, what I'm looking at, what I'm seeing and
what it means, what I want and what I'm afraid of.*

Joan Didion[2]

Within this book, each of the eight cardinal points of the Compass represents an aspect of how you can ignite, grow and/or sustain your creativity. An overview of *'The Compass Rose'* is shown on the next page.

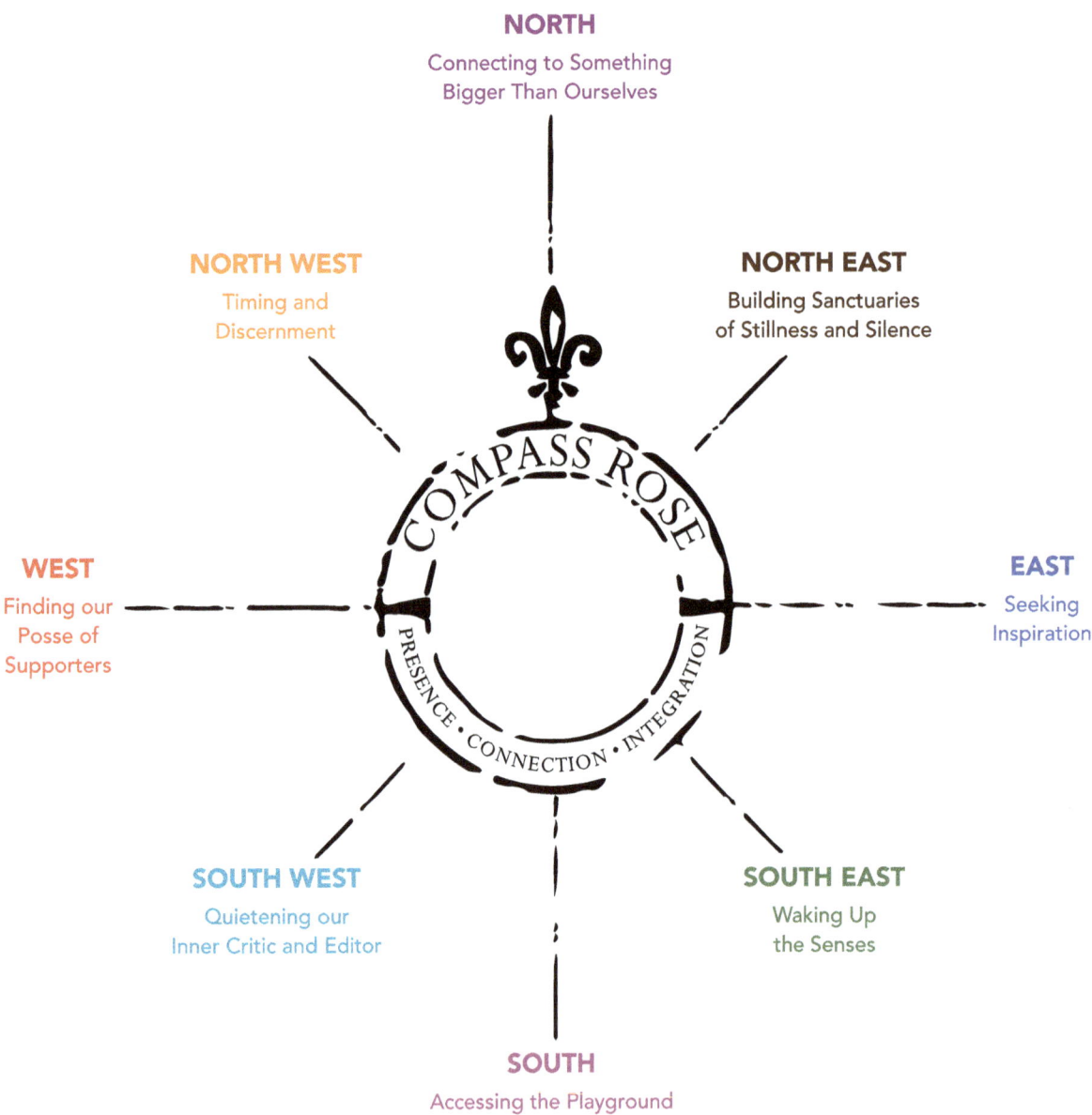

How to Use This Book

We have chosen the metaphor of the Compass because at the centre of a compass is a balance point which is called the Rose. The more finely calibrated the Rose is, the 'better' – more finely tuned – the Compass is. A Compass cannot tell you where to go but the better adjusted it is, the better it will pick up tiny shifts in your direction in order to be more accurate about where you actually are. From there you can ensure your course stays true. Looking after your inner compass is looking after yourself.

In this Workbook there will be a description of each cardinal point, with prompts and a couple of questions to stimulate your personal reflection.

The eight cardinal points are as follows:

- North East: Building Sanctuaries of Stillness and Silence
- East: Seeking Inspiration
- South East: Waking Up the Senses
- South: Accessing the Playground of our Inner Resources
- South West: Quietening Our Inner Critic and Editor
- West: Finding our Posse of Supporters
- North West: Timing and Discernment
- North: Connecting to Something Bigger than Ourselves

You may also find you have questions of your own that will arise spontaneously as you work with each of the cardinal points. Give yourself a little time to journal what thoughts, feelings and sensations arise. They can offer you treasure. Trust your intuition and go with the flow of what calls without letting your inner editor put you off. You can always go back and re-read, change or alter what you capture, but the key is allowing your first ideas and thoughts to flow onto the blank page of your journal.

At the end of each reflection, follow the invitation to circle one word and then move onto the next cardinal point. At the end of visiting all eight points we return to the heart centre of the Rose with a practice which is described on page 27.

Let your heart be your compass, your mind your map, your soul your guide and you will never get lost.

Ritu Ghatourey[3]

Before you Begin

Start with wherever you are. Take a moment to sit quietly and relax into the space you have created to work with your Compass. With any good Compass as you stand holding it you need to be still, so that you get an accurate reading. Take time to centre your energy so you are grounded. Pay attention to your breath as a way for you to become present to the moment.

When you are ready ask yourself:

- What do I want to explore today concerning my creativity?
- What wants to be known here?

Take a few minutes to capture your thoughts in your journal or in the space provided here.

We start with the North East cardinal point but you are welcome to start at wherever feels right for you.

Ask to know what you are born to do.
Follow the compass of joy.

Barbara Marx Hubbard[5]

COMPASS ROSE

PRESENCE · CONNECTION · INTEGRATION

How to Use This Book

Visiting the Eight Cardinal Points of The Compass Rose

Your *Creativity* Compass

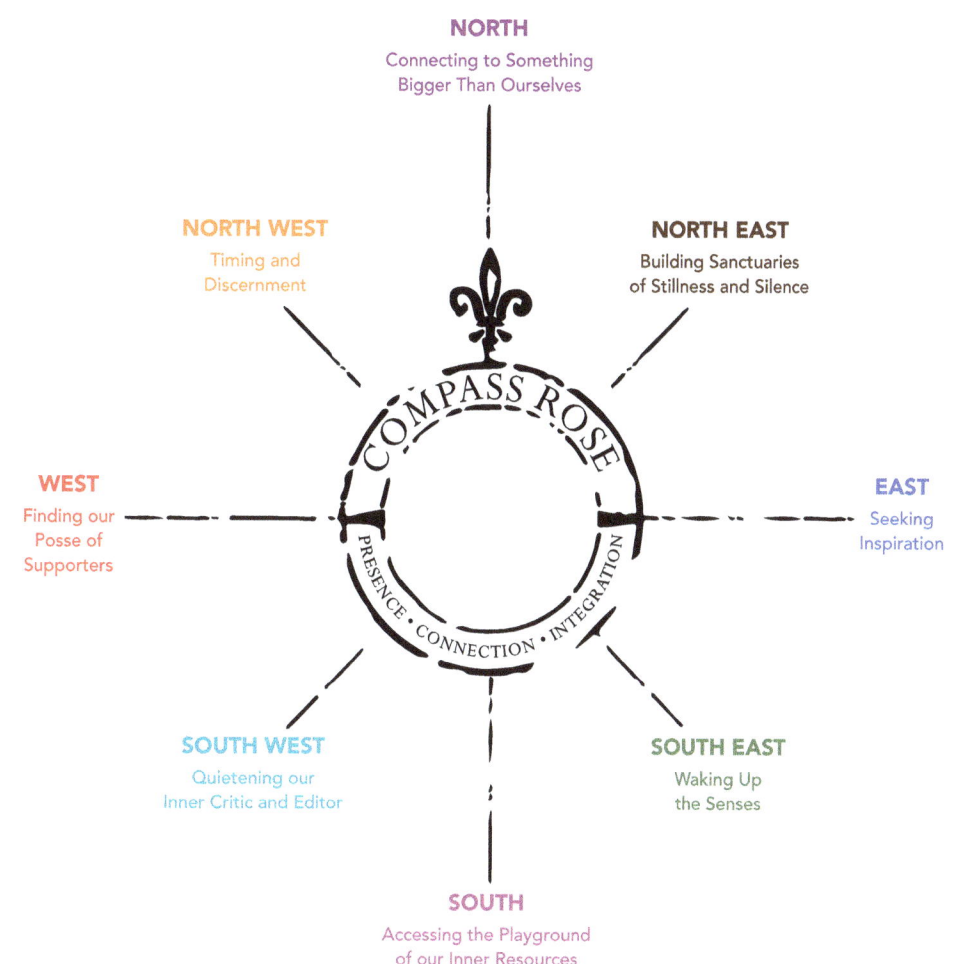

NORTH
Connecting to Something Bigger Than Ourselves

NORTH EAST
Building Sanctuaries of Stillness and Silence

EAST
Seeking Inspiration

SOUTH EAST
Waking Up the Senses

SOUTH
Accessing the Playground of our Inner Resources

SOUTH WEST
Quietening our Inner Critic and Editor

WEST
Finding our Posse of Supporters

NORTH WEST
Timing and Discernment

NORTH EAST

The Cardinal Direction: North East
Building Sanctuaries of Stillness and Silence

Within you there is a stillness and a sanctuary that you can retreat to at any time and be yourself.

Hermann Hesse[6]

When you hear the word 'sanctuary' what comes to mind? It might be in your own home, a room or a corner chair sitting in the stillness of morning sunlight or sitting by the fireside glow on a winter's evening. For some, it is a place in nature and for others it is a café with a favourite table where they can write. Public or private, however tiny, it is the sense of a place that is away from the crowds, whether they are in our head or out in the world. It is a place of solace where we can feel especially safe, so that we can refresh and resource – a place of retreat that holds some special energy for you where you feel held. We know that creating our own sanctuary or sanctuaries helps our creativity to flourish.

Take some time to reflect on what a sanctuary might be for you.

- How can you create the time, places, and spaces you need to wholeheartedly support and nurture your creativity?
- How might you need to seek out or ask for what I need?

Take a few minutes to jot down what arises when you read these two questions. When you have finished look back over what you have written and circle one word that especially stands out for you as a key word. Perhaps a couple of words call to you – that's fine too.

My word is:

EAST

The Cardinal Direction: East
Seeking Inspiration

Anything can be creative.
You bring that quality to the activity.

Osho[7]

What inspires you? What gives you hope and a sense of excitement? Is it something you read? Is it a kind of music? One song perhaps? Is it the energy of a group of like-minded souls or ringfencing time alone in some naturally beautiful spot? Where do you go to get a regular dose of inspiration? Actively seeking out sources of inspiration regularly keeps us vibrant, interested, awake and alive. Finding unexpected places to refresh provides inspiration which lies dormant deep within us. We know the joy and the inspiration we get from being open to finding the extraordinary in ordinary.

And so,

- How might you fill your well of inspiration?
- What is unfamiliar or different that could transport you away from your normal sights, routine or sources of inspiration?

Now take a few minutes to jot down what arises when you read these two questions. When you have finished look back over what you have written and circle one word that especially stands out for you as a key word. Perhaps a couple might call to you – that's fine too.

My word is:

The Cardinal Direction: South East
Waking Up the Senses

You must learn to heed your senses. Humans use but a tiny percentage of theirs…. but they talk. Oh, do they talk.

Michael Scott[8]

Our senses are a wonderful portal to our natural creativity. If we follow our senses, we can continually open ourselves up to fresh experiences and discoveries which may fuel our creativity. Many times, the pressure to rush means we do not gift ourselves this opportunity to slow down and savour the senses we have. We invite you take some time away from the Compass Map and conduct a personal experiment to see which of your senses are strongest, which speak to you with information which you might need to enlist in the service of your developing creativity. As regular walkers, we appreciate how being immersed in nature with our senses fully alive gifts us new ideas and new perspectives.

One way to do this is to choose a place outdoors for a nature walk to experiment. Is your hearing the strongest sense? Really tune in and listen without filtering. Try silence and the absence of sound too. What aromas are around you? Another approach would be to spend a little time with your spice cabinet, or at a perfume counter or breathe in deeply the scent of a wood or park. Take time to really taste what you have in the next meal. Experiment with touching different textures. What do you see? Then take your pen and try one of these questions to reflect:

- How and what do you notice?

- Which of the senses do you rely on above the others? How might you be able to create more of a balance to get a fuller experience?

Now, take a few minutes to jot down what arises when you read these two questions. When you have finished, look back over what you have written and circle one word that especially stands out for you as a key word. Perhaps a couple might call to you – that's fine too.

My word is:

SOUTH

The Cardinal Direction: South
Accessing the Playground of our Inner Resources

Play keeps us alive and vital. It gives us enthusiasm for life that is irreplaceable. Without it, life just does not taste so good.

Lucia Capocchione[9]

If there is one specific area where creativity gets a boost, it is when we let play in and give ourselves permission to dare, get messy, make mistakes and play for play's sake. This is a precursor to a light-hearted approach, joy and an important aspect of following our interest of cultivating curiosity and letting our heart's wisdom express itself. An atmosphere of playfulness helps people to find their way back to their creativity and enhances motivation. In this way we can let ourselves be enchanted by the extraordinary in the ordinary everyday world. When we let ourselves make mistakes and just have a go, it exponentially shows up in what we do. We realise in our life and work the release that permission to play can joyfully feed into our creativity.

And so, do you take time enough to play?

- How do you connect with your inner child? What permissions do you give yourself to really play, have fun and experiment?
- How do you tune into the wisdom of your heart?

Now, take a few minutes to jot down what arises when you read these questions. When you have finished look back over what you have written and circle one word that especially stands out for you as a key word. Perhaps a couple might call to you – that's fine too.

My word is:

SOUTH WEST

The Cardinal Direction: South West
Quietening your Inner Critic and Editor

*Say goodbye to your inner critic and
take this pledge to be kinder to yourself*

Oprah Winfrey[10]

Creativity means moving out of our comfort zone and risking ourselves in some way. And at just these times our inner critic or editor wants to hold us back, keep us safe, stop our playing or criticise our experimentation. As we play, we need to invite our inner critic to step to one side to clear our way to just 'be' and allow our creativity to simply flow through us. And we also need to reassure our inner critic that there is a time for careful compassionate editing when we come – downstream – to the crafting stage of the creativity process. And this allows space for other wiser voices to be heard. The importance of maintaining a loving dialogue from our own experiences is priceless.

And so, to support yourself here ask yourself:

- How might I be able to befriend my inner critic?
- How might my inner critic need to be comforted so I am freer to explore?

Now take a few minutes to jot down what arises when you read these two questions. When you have finished look back over what you have written and circle one word that especially stands out for you as a key word. Perhaps a couple might call to you – that's fine too.

My word is:

The Cardinal Direction: West
Finding our Posse of Supporters

Life is not a solo act. It's a huge collaboration, and we all need to assemble around us the people who care about us and support us.

Tim Gunn[11]

Creative endeavour can be a lonely road as we hunker down and give ourselves over to making, crafting, designing and planning. Having people to draw upon as sources of support and inspiration can be very important. If you were to make a list of those who have helped you along your creative way, who would be on it? Maybe they did not even know at the time that they were a source of inspiration. Maybe it is someone you have never met but their writing, music or art influenced you. Maybe it is someone you knew when you were young who believed in you more than you did and who is no longer around for you to thank today. It could be people you know now or those you look to who have been teachers or who are just there to say, 'keep going.' We know from our own experience how important it is to have our own posse of supporters who want to just encourage us both individually and together to 'keep going'.

And so, ask yourself:

- Who are the people who will support and encourage me in my creative endeavours?
- What new friends, networks or resources might I need to further support me?

Now take a few minutes to jot down what arises when you read these two questions. When you have finished look back over what you have written and circle one word that especially stands out for you as a key word. Perhaps a couple might call to you – that's fine too.

My word is:

NORTH WEST

Vulnerability	Resiliance		Excitement
Boldness	Playfulness		Tenderness
Understanding	Appreciation	Serenity	Integrity
Willingness	Energy		Consistency
Choice Love	Experience	Gratitude	Responsibility
Empowerment	Void		Honesty
Support Contentment	Education	Confidence	Recognition
Simplicity	Engagement		Adaptability

??????????

The Cardinal Direction: North West
Timing and Discernment

Courage starts with showing up and letting ourselves be seen.
Brene Bown[12]

Do you want to be courageous with your creativity – or start small? What quality will help you along? If we want to be courageous a leap to 100 per cent more of any quality is a tall order in a busy schedule. So, begin by building small. 5% is a doable positive start and the good thing is this can grow and grow. If you were to have 5% more of a particular quality, what would it be and what would it give you? If you woke up tomorrow with 5% more of that quality, how would you know it was alive and well in you? Start slowly. We love this gentle practice because it is both practical and achievable – and 5% of something is often all we need to shift our energies.

And so as you pick one of the qualities on the previous page or choose whatever you know is right for you right now.

- What do you need 5 per cent more of to honour your creativity?
- How can you learn to trust your instincts and intuitions more as you craft your ideas and offer them out into the world?

Now, take a few minutes to jot down what arises when you read these two questions. When you have finished look back over what you have written and circle one word that especially stands out for you as a key word. Perhaps a couple might call to you – that's fine too.

My word is:

The Cardinal Direction: North
Connecting to Something Bigger than Ourselves

The soul is the truth of who you are.

Marianne Williamson[13]

This direction is about tuning into ways we 'know' things. Generally speaking, individuals have their own specific ideas about what 'knowledge' looks like. This is fine, but it can mean that other important ways of knowing fall fallow for lack of consideration. It can be easy to stay with the habitual ways of knowing and experiment with different ways of knowing and accessing inner wisdom.

And so, take time to ask yourself two key questions:

- What is my creativity asking of me?
- What does my soul want me to know?

You can do this seated, or standing up to get some energy to flow. Start wherever you wish.

- Put your hands on your heart and take a few moments to connect to your heart and ask the key question: **'What does my heart have to say about this question?'**
- Then put your hands on your solar plexus and ask, **'What does my gut have to say about the question?'**
- Then open your arms and hands to the side of your body and ask, **'What does my body know about this question and what does my creativity want from me?'**
- Finally, put your hands on your head and ask, **'What thoughts do I have about the question?'**

Take a few minutes to jot down what arises when you read these two questions. When you have finished look back over what you have written and circle one word that especially stands out for you as a key word. Perhaps a couple might call to you – that's fine too.

My word is:

Harvesting

Happiness is the harvest of a quiet eye.

Austin O'Malley [14]

By now you will have visited all eight of the cardinal directions of the Compass. Regardless of where you began, this will be the last point because here is where you harvest your experiences.

Along the way we hope you have gathered thoughts, reflections, sensations and feelings.

If you also did the word gathering exercise that follows each of the other seven points you will have circled 8 stand-out words. Put those words in a list and take a moment to look them over.

Now returning to the centre of the Compass Rose we return to the central practices of Presence, Connection and Integration. We connect to this presencing by grounding, centring our energy and taking a moment to focus on our in and out breaths, taking a slightly longer exhale as we do so, aligning ourself with our mind, body and soul and then asking ourself as we look over our eight words:

- For Connection: 'What am I connecting to now?' and 'What is making sense for me right now?'
- For Integration: 'What can I take forward?'

From this place is there is one word that stands out from all the rest? Anything when you think back to the original question, topic or focus for your travelling the points of the compass? Perhaps you are attracted to some or all of them?

Now consider how together these can help you resource your creativity. Use the words that you have to write for a few minutes which could turn out to be a promise to yourself, some words of inspiration or a fresh road map for you and your creativity.

My circled words are:

My Road Map for growing my creativity is:

Your Onward Journey

We hope you have enjoyed working with *The Compass Rose – 8 Ways to Awaken your Creativity and Re-Source your Life and your Practice*.

For more inspiration, please read our books 'Nature's Way – Designing the Life you Want through the Lens of Nature and the Five Seasons' and 'Reflect to Create! The Dance of Reflection for Creative Leadership, Professional Practice and Supervision' and do please join us on our Creativity Programme *'Cultivating and Choreographing the Rich Tapestry of Wholehearted Creativity'* which is an EMCC Global EQA Accredited Virtual 12-month Inquiry into how you can learn how to re-Source Yourself as you re-Vitalise your Practice.

For more information, do not hesitate to contact us at
karyn@fletcherprentice.com or elaine@reflect2create.com

References, Further Resources and Reading

Here is some further reading to inspire you:

On Creativity

Allan, D. (2002) *What If! – Sticky Wisdom, How to Start a Creative Revolution at Work.* Chichester, Capston

Atavar, M. (2011) *12 Rules of Creativity.* London, Kiosk Publishing

Beek, E. (2019) *Mindful Thoughts for Makers – Connecting head, heart, hands.* UK, Leaping Hare Press

Brown, B. (2010) *The Gifts of Imperfection – Let Go of Who You Think You're Supposed to Be and Embrace Who You Are. Your Guide to Wholehearted Living.* Minnesota, Hazelden

Cameron, J. (1994) *The Artist's Way – A Course in Discovering and Recovering Your Creative Self.* London, Pan Books

Chodron, P. (2001) *Start Where You Are – A Guide to Compassionate Living.* USA, Shambhala Publications

Gelb, M. J. (2014) *Creativity on Demand – How to Ignite and Sustain the Fire of Genius.* USA, California

Gilbert, E. (2015) *Big Magic – Creative Living Beyond Fear.* London, Bloomsbury Publishing

Gompertz, W. (2015) *Think Like An Artist – and Lead a More Creative, Productive Life.* UK, Penguin Random House

Hegatary, J. (2018) *Hegarty on Creativity – There Are No Rules.* London, Thames & Hudson Ltd.

Hershey, T. (2015) *Sanctuary Creating a Space for Grace in Your Life.* Chicago, Loyola Press

Johnson, A. (2001) *Leaving a Trace – On Keeping a Journal.* New York, Little Brown and Company

Judkins, R. (2015) *The Art of Creative Thinking.* London, Hodder & Stoughton Ltd.

Lamott, A. (1994) *Bird By Bird – Some Instructions on Writing and Life.* New York Anchor Books

Maisel, E. (2005) *Coaching the Artist Within.* USA, New World Library

Maisel, E. (2019) *Inside Creativity Coaching.* London, Routledge

Osho (1999) *Creativity – Unleashing the Forces Within.* New York, Osho International Foundation

Patterson, E. (2019) *Reflect to Create! The Dance of Reflection for Creative Leadership, Professional Practice and Supervision.* London, Centre for Reflection and Creativity Ltd.

Shapiro, D. (2013) *Still Writing – The Perils and Pleasures of a Creative Life.* US Grove Press

Udall, N. (2014) *Riding the Creative Rollercoaster – How Leaders Evoke Creativity, Productivity and Innovation.* London, Kogan Page

On Nature

Beer, A. (2020) *Every Day Nature – How Noticing Nature Can Quietly Change your Life.* London, National Trust

Benyus, J. (2002) *Biomimicry – Innovation Inspired by Nature.* New York, Harper Perennial

Crumley, J. (2017) *The Nature of the Seasons Series.* UK, Saraband

Ford, A. (2017) *Mindful Thoughts for Walkers – Footnotes on the Zen Path.* UK, Leaping Hare Press

Harrison, M. (editor) (2016) Seasons (a 4-volume anthology) . UK, The Wildlife Trusts

Hershey, T. (2000) *Soul Gardening – Cultivating the Good Life.* Minneapolis, Augsburg Fortress

Kimmerer, R. W. (2013) *Braiding Sweetgrass – Ingenious Wisdom, Scientific Knowledge and the Teachings of Plants.* USA Penguin

Louv, R. (2012) *The Nature Principle – Reconnecting with Life in a Virtual Age.* North Carolina, Algonquin Books of Chapel Hill

Prentice, K. (2020) *Nature's Way – Designing the Life you Want through the Lens of Nature and the Five Seasons.* Cambridgeshire, Fletcher Prentice Associates

On Stilling the Space

Ford, A. (2011) *The Art of Mindful Walking*. East Sussex, Leaping Hare Press

Harris, M. (2017) *Solitude – in Pursuit of a Singular Life in a Crowded World*. London, Random House Books

Kunditz, D. (1998) *Stopping – How to be Still When You Have to Keep Going*. California, Conari Press

Miller, B. & Hughes, H. (2012) *The Pen and the Bell – Mindful Writing in a Busy World*. Boston Skinner House Books

Penman, D. (2015) *Mindfulness for Creativity – Adapt, Create and Thrive in a Frantic World*. London, Piatkus

Read, M. (2014) *Slowing Down in a Speed Stressed World*. USA, Life Press

Sunim, Haemin & Kim, Chi-Young. (2018) *The Things You Can See Only When You Slow Down*. London, Penguin

From the World of Poetry and Prose

Foster, J. (2013) *Falling in Love with Where You Are – A Year of Prose and Poetry on Radically Opening Up to the Pain and Joy of Life*. Salisbury, Non-Duality Press

O'Donohue, J. (2015) *Walking in Wonder – Eternal Wisdom for a Modern World*. New York, Crown Publishers

Oliver, M. (2017) *Devotions – The Selected Poems of Mary Oliver*. London, Penguin Press

Oliver, M. (2019) *A Thousand Mornings*. USA, Corsair Publishing

Barks, C. (trans) (2007) *Rumi's Bridge to the Soul, Journeys into the Music and Silence of the Heart*. New York, Harper Collins

Stafford, W. (2014) *Ask Me – 100 Essential Poems*. USA, Graywolf Press

Whyte, D. (2007) *Many Rivers Flow*. Langley, Many Rivers Press

Picture References

Some photos and all the graphics are the authors own. All other photos and quotes are in the public domain and are courtesy of Unsplash, © Adobe Stock and www.goodreads.com respectively.

[1]   *'Barbara Sher Quotes.' Quoteslyfe.com*, 2022. Wed. 14 Dec. 2022. www.quoteslyfe.com/quote/Your-creativity-is-waiting-for-you-like-398933

[2]   Didion, J. (1968) 'On Keeping a Notebook,' essay included in *Slouching Towards Bethlehem*. USA. Fourth Estate

[3]   Downloaded 14th December 2022 from www.goodreads.com

[4]   Downloaded 14th December 2022 from www.searchquotes.com

[5]   Downloaded 14th December 2022 from www.goodreads.com

[6-14] Quotes throughout from www.goodreads.com or www.brainyquote.com

*You can't use up creativity.
The more you use, the more you have.*

Maya Angelou

About Elaine and Karyn

We are **Elaine Patterson** and **Karyn Prentice** and together we are the internationally award-winning PattersonPrenticeDesigns.

This unique design partnership brings our shared love of the arts, nature, creativity, reflection and writing to the worlds of Executive Reflection, Coaching Supervision, Leadership and Professional Practice. Together we design and host uniquely heart-based, soulful and somatic creative reflective learning experiences both online and in beautiful places across the world.

We are internationally accredited Executive Coaches, Coaching Supervisors, OD Specialists and published authors and from October 2019 to 2022 we co-led the delivery of the Coaching Supervision Academy's International Diploma in Coaching Supervision in London. Karyn's book *Nature's Way: Designing the Life You Want through the Lens of Nature and the Five Seasons* and Elaine's book *Reflect to Create! The Dance of Reflection for Creative Leadership, Professional Practice and Supervision* are available on Amazon and Waterstones.

Together, we delight in co-hosting our flagship EMCC Global EQA Accredited Diploma *Cultivating and Choreographing the Rich Tapestry of Wholehearted Creativity* which is a virtual 12-month Inquiry to re-Source You and re-Vitalize your Professional Life and *Bridging the Unknown: From Role Work to Soul Calling in Later Life* which is a virtual 9 month inquiry into the invitations which open up to us in later life.

For more information, please visit Karyn's website at www.fletcherprentice.com and Elaine's at www.centreforreflectionandcreativity.org

www.ingramcontent.com/pod-product-compliance
Lightning Source LLC
Chambersburg PA
CBHW051332110526
44590CB00032B/4491